{{code creation}}

T0102023

CODING ACTIVITIES FOR
BUILDING
DATABASES
WITH SQL

Sarah Mullin

ROSEN
PUBLISHING

Published in 2022 by The Rosen Publishing Group, Inc.
29 East 21st Street, New York, NY 10010

Library of Congress Cataloging-in-Publication Data

Names: Mullin, Sarah, author.
Title: Coding activities for building databases with SQL / Sarah Mullin.
Description: First edition. | New York : Rosen Publishing,
2022. | Series: Code creator | Audience: Grades 7–12. |
Includes bibliographical references and index.
Identifiers: LCCN 2019011068| ISBN 9781725340992
(library bound) | ISBN 9781725340985 (pbk.)
Subjects: LCSH: SQL (Computer program language)—Juvenile literature.
| Database design—Juvenile literature. | Databases—Juvenile literature.
Classification: LCC QA76.73.S67 M85 2022 | DDC 005.75/6—dc23
LC record available at https://lccn.loc.gov/2019011068

Manufactured in the United States of America

Some of the images in this book illustrate individuals who are models. The depictions
do not imply actual situations or events.

CPSIA Compliance Information: Batch #CSRYA22. For further information contact Rosen Publishing, New York, New York at 1-800-237-9932.

Find us on

Contents

Introduction

Data consists of facts that need to be processed to gain information about something. For instance, here are some facts: a man has an opened umbrella, a woman is wearing a rain jacket, puddles are on the ground, and the man and the woman are in the same location. Processing those facts, it is possible to gain the information that it is raining. Data is constantly being produced in the world, both by official agencies and regular, everyday people. When someone goes to the doctor's office, nurses collect information about their health and store it in electronic health records. When someone shops online, the items on the site and the items they purchase become data. Data is everywhere.

How is all this data stored? A database allows someone to store data related to some topic in an organized way. It has to be well organized so that the database owners can use the data to make decisions and find patterns. Data can be stored in a variety of ways, ranging from very simple tables to complex database design. The way data is stored depends on many factors: the type of data it is, the size of the data, and how complex the data is. Data is commonly organized in rows—called records—with each column containing a piece of data for that record. The simplest database, a flat file database, is a single table that can store a limited amount of data. These are typically files that have one record per line and each column is separated by a delimiter. Delimiters can be commas, tabs, spaces, and many other characters. For instance, comma-separated value (CSV) files store data that is separated by commas.

However, data stored in separate files can create problems with inconsistent data formats, data that does not have any

Data—and lots of it—is everywhere; it can be stored in an organized way by designing a database.

relationships across files, and data that does not have any rules or constraints. In addition to these problems, there is also big data—huge quantities of data of all types. What does someone do if they have a lot of data that cannot be put all in one table? Relational databases link multiple tables together using an index or key field. This allows users to easily find records from search criteria across the tables.

Relational databases require a database management system (DBMS) to manage and access data. Data in these types of databases tends to be structured, meaning that data can be defined as data types that are easily searchable. Object-relational databases are a combination of object-orientated databases and relational databases. What about data that is not easily searchable, like social media posts, text messages, music, images, or videos? This data is unstructured and typically stored in NoSQL or non-relational databases.

However, the most beginner-friendly format is structured data. What does that look like? Structured data consists of numerical information, data that can be organized on a scale, or data that can be organized in categories. Data can be entered by machines; automatically generated by computer processes, applications, or other mechanisms without the help of humans; or entered by humans. Machine-generated data is used in mobile cell phone logs, manufacturing field equipment performance, and medical devices that collect

Database management systems offer a way to efficiently manage, store, and retrieve data from databases.

health information. Human-entered data can be entered manually and includes things like answers on quizzes, where someone lives, and birthdates.

Databases consist of data in two forms: records and metadata. The latter is data that describes how the database is set up and the relationships among the data. A DBMS is responsible for creating, managing, and retrieving information, as well as acting to manage and interact with a group of databases. A DBMS also has data in the form of metadata and operational data, which includes data dictionaries, relationships to other records and objects, and administrative information. DBMS software uses database languages to access, modify, store, and retrieve data. One such database language is Structured Query Language (SQL), which will be used in these exercises.

SQL is a language that allows users to create databases, add new data, and query data from them. It is composed of statements that perform certain types of data manipulation and administration; it allows users to create objects and define them, and transform and modify the data. SQL is used to communicate with relational databases—you tell SQL what you want and how to get what you want from the database. These activities will use PostgreSQL, an object-relational database management system, and the SQL database language.

In the following exercises, your goal is to help save the world by designing a database for Mithras—a secret government agency—and querying the database for Jupiter, the head of the agency. Jupiter has asked you to keep a record of the missions, supplies, money, and agents that will allow anyone with clearance in Mithras to easily query and gain data from the database.

SQL allows users to store, query, and manipulate data in an effective and organized way. This is highly important in commercial applications.

To get started with database management, head to the PostgreSQL site (https://www.postgresql.org/download) and download the binary packages. The download option will depend on the operating system on your computer: Windows, MacOS, or Linux. Select the appropriate system and follow the instructions to get the download started. Once PostgreSQL is downloaded and installed, start the interactive terminal program—called psql—which allows users to run SQL commands and create databases. Open a terminal window and type:

psql postgres

The command to quit this program is \q, and the command to get help is \help. After initializing the terminal program, it is time to create the Mithras database. The CREATE DATABASE command is used to do this:

postgres=# CREATE DATABASE Mithras;
CREATE DATABASE
postgres=#

After typing in this command, make sure to end it with a semi-colon character. Once the Mithras database has been created, users can be added by using the CREATE USER command, as follows:

postgres=# CREATE USER agent1;
CREATE ROLE

To check for databases, use the command \list or \l. Either of these commands will return a list of databases. To list all of the users, use the command \du, which will return a list of users (for now, it is only agent1).
Now, quit out of psql and login to the Mithras database:

psql Mithras agent1;

To set a password for agent1, type \password agent1. When asked to enter a password, enter "databasefun123!" The agent1 user now has this as the required password.
All commands in the following exercises can be done in psql. It is also possible to use the Atom package "data-atom," DataGrip, pgAdmin 4, or another platform for databases and SQL that help visualize data easier.

To use Atom, make sure the "data-atom" package is installed. Then, go to Packages> Data Atom>New connection and enter the following information:

New Connection...

Connection	PostgreSQL11.2	Or	PostgreSQL11.2
URL	postgresql://agent1:databasefun123!@localhost/Mithras		
DB Type	PostgreSQL		
Server	localhost	Port	5432
Auth	agent1	databasefun123!	
Database	Mithras		
Options	option=value,ssl=true		

Connect   Save and Connect   Close

This image shows the creation of a new connection to your database in Atom, an interactive development environment.

Once that is entered, click on Save and Connect. With all this in place, you should be ready to start on these activities. Keep in mind that it is possible to execute SQL commands and see the database in action by accessing the Execute tab under the package "data-atom."

Activity 1

Designing a Database

The accuracy and usefulness of a database is dependent on the level of detail and information in the database design. Jupiter—head of Mithras—produces a lot of data, so it is necessary to figure out how to design the new secret agency's database in a way that makes the most sense for the agency's needs.

A database works by storing information in tables, each of which is made up of rows and columns. A row represents a record and a column represents an attribute. For example:

Supplies	Category	Quantity
Camera Glasses	Gadget	10
Surveillance Drone	Gadget	5
Motorcycle	Vehicle	2

A record is a representation of some object, such as a person's bank account. Each person at the bank is assigned a record and each record has multiple attributes, such as name, address, savings accounts, and money transactions. In the above table, the attributes are Supplies, Category, and Quantity. Each row represents a supply item, the category the item fits into, and the amount of each item. The table has three rows and therefore, it has three records.

A database schema is the overall organization of all the tables in a database with limits on the type of data that can be stored in the tables. A relational database schema introduces relationships between tables and is designed to reduce repeated or unnecessary information. This means that data is divided among tables and there is not much overlapping information. For example, there would not be one table that had Supplies, Category, and Quantity, and another table that had Supplies, Category, Quantity, and Cost— because one table can be derived from the other.

With that background knowledge, it is time to get to work. Jupiter has supplied information about the Mithras agents, including their skills and other physical characteristics. He has also provided information about the Mithras missions for each agent and the supplies they have used on each of these missions.

Focus on the first table of the database and call it "agent." Each agent's information package contains his or her name, height, and hair color. In addition, five skills have been tested for the agents: Technology, Intelligence, Speed, Communication, and Protection. These five skills are graded on a scale from 1 to 5.

To organize all of this information into a table, the first step is to create one record for each agent, where a row represents an agent and all of the data that belongs to them. Finally, an identification attribute needs to be assigned to each agent. For simplicity, each AgentID will be one number that can be used to uniquely identify each agent. Below is a table organizing all this data:

AgentID	AgentName	Height(inches)	HairColor	Technology	Intelligence	Speed	Communication	Protection
1	Mars	77	Red	4	4	2	4	5
2	Neptune	72	Blue	5	3	5	1	2
3	Diana	64	Yellow	4	5	5	2	5
4	Minerva	60	Purple	4	5	1	5	3

Activity 2

Using SQL and Creating an Agent Table

It is now time to enter the agent information table into the Mithras database. A typical table is defined like this:

CREATE TABLE <table name>
(
AttributeName, Datatype, Optional Attribute Constraint,
AttributeName, Datatype, Optional Attribute Constraint,
Optional table Constraints
);

    CREATE TABLE is the SQL command to initiate a table in a database. Since the goal is to create a table with the agents in it, the <table name> should be "agent." Next, remember that attributes should describe the records. What are the attributes (or columns) in the table? It is important to describe the agents by their identification numbers, names, height, hair color, and their specific skills. So, replace AttributeName with the names of these attributes, like so:

CREATE TABLE agent (
    AgentID Datatype Optional Attribute Constraint,
    AgentName Datatype Optional Attribute Constraint,
    Height Datatype Optional Attribute Constraint,
    HairColor Datatype Optional Attribute Constraint,
    Technology Datatype Optional Attribute Constraint,
    Intelligence Datatype Optional Attribute Constraint,
    Speed Datatype Optional Attribute Constraint,
    Communication Datatype Optional Attribute Constraint,
    Protection Datatype Optional Attribute Constraint,
    );

The Datatype element here is used to define what kind of values these attributes can take. They can be broken down into numeric, date and time, character, and binary. Within these types there are also subtypes. Some data types in SQL are:

- Numeric
  - o Bit: Integer data, or a whole number, that is represented with a 0 or 1
  - o Int: Integer data from –2,147,483,648 to 2,147,483,648
  - o Float: Fractional data that can have numbers on either side of a decimal point
- Datetime
  - o Datetime: Date and time data, from January 1, 1753, to December 31, 9999
- Character
  - o Char: Fixed-length character data that can be 8000 characters long
  - o Varchar: Variable-length character data that can be up to 8000 characters long
  - o Text: Variable-length character data that has a maximum length of 2,147,483,647

Now, think about the agent data. The attributes AgentName and HairColor are character data types—they contain information that is only made up of combinations of characters. The next question to ask is whether they have to be a fixed length or if they have a length that varies. Is Mars the same number of characters as Minerva? No—Mars is four characters and Minerva is seven characters. To use storage space efficiently, these attributes should be given the data type varchar. It will also be useful to set the size of the variable by figuring out the maximum number of characters that variable could have. Since AgentName is only considering code names, the maximum number of characters should not be too high—perhaps a limit of fifteen characters will be sufficient.

What about the height attribute? Height is included in the table as inches, which can be represented in whole numbers. Therefore, the attribute's data type should be int. A similar procedure will also apply to the skill attributes. The agents' attributes were measured and rated on a scale of 1 to 5. Therefore, the variables can only take on the numbers 1, 2, 3, 4, or 5. Thus, they can be assigned the data type smallint. This is a variation of the int data type that is useful for smaller numbers. Using smallint instead of int will help save space, which is valuable for any database.

Finally, it is time to decide if the attributes have any Optional Attribute Constraints. These are: NULL, NOT NULL, UNIQUE, and PRIMARY KEY. The attribute constraints NULL and NOT NULL have to do with missing data. How can data be missing, one may ask? For example, say Jupiter forgot to record the height of Mars, but still has the rest of his information. In the Mithras database, every other data point can be recorded, and the Height attribute can simply be NULL—because it is "missing."

If the NULL constraint is used, it means that a record can be created without a value for this attribute. If the constraint NOT NULL is used, it means that a record must have a value for this attribute when it is created.

A PRIMARY KEY identifies the unique record identifier for the table. In this case, the unique record identifier for the database will be AgentID, since everything will be linked to an agent, including missions they go on and supplies they need.

The UNIQUE constraint is used to disallow duplicate values in the column. Would Jupiter want two agents with the same code name? That could become confusing. The AgentName attribute should require a unique name that represents only one agent and not multiple agents.

Now, revisit the CREATE TABLE statement and enter all that information:

```
CREATE TABLE agent (
        AgentID int NOT NULL PRIMARY KEY,
        AgentName varchar(15) NOT NULL UNIQUE,
        Height int NULL,
        HairColor varchar(20) NULL,
        Technology smallint,
        Intelligence smallint,
        Speed smallint,
        Communication smallint,
        Protection smallint
        );
```

Congratulations—this input should have created an agent table that incorporates different data types and constraints.

Activity 3

Inserting Data into a Database Table

Now that there is a table schema that has attribute names, data types, and constraints, things can really get moving. Run a query for SELECT * FROM agent. Is there anything in the table? No—the table is empty and only contains the attribute names.

```
Query:
 1   SELECT * FROM agent;

Results:

   agentid  agentname  height  haircolor  technology  intelligence  speed  communication  protection
```

All of these attributes for agents Mars, Neptune, Diana, Minerva, Venus, and Pluto exist—so how do they make it into the table created? How is a record for each of the agents with their ID, names, height, hair color, and skills created? To put records in the table, it is necessary to use the INSERT INTO command.

Start off by putting a record for Mars into the table. Jupiter has provided this information from the original table: agent Mars has AgentID: 1, AgentName: Mars, Height: 77, HairColor: Red, Technology: 4, Intelligence: 4, Speed: 2, Communication: 4, and Protection: 5

In general, inserting these values is done with a statement written like this:

INSERT INTO table VALUES (attribute values for the record);

In this format, the table is "agent" and the record values correspond to the values for each of Mars's attributes. The VALUES component identifies that different values are going to be entered for each of these attributes. Each of the values is separated by a comma to indicate it belongs in a different attribute—without the commas, things would get confusing, fast. Character data types—like varchar—need to be inside single quotation marks. Finally, the order of the values needs to be the same as the table schema created in the earlier activities. Here is how it looks for Mars:

INSERT INTO agent VALUES (1, 'Mars', 77, 'Red', 4, 4, 2, 4, 5);

Putting all of the agent information into the table one line at a time can be tiring. Instead, try putting the rest of the records in one statement:

INSERT INTO agent (AgentID, AgentName, Height, HairColor, Technology, Intelligence, Speed, Communication, Protection)

VALUES
(2, 'Neptune', 72, 'Blue', 5, 3, 5, 1, 2),
(3, 'Diana', 64, 'Yellow', 4, 5, 5, 2, 5),
(4, 'Minerva', 60, 'Purple', 4, 5, 1, 5, 3),
(5, 'Venus', 61, 'Red', 2, 4, 2, 5, 4),
(6, 'Pluto', NULL, 'Purple', 4, 4, 4, 4, 4);

Here, the first statement is defining the names of the attributes that will be inserted. To insert data for all of the attributes in a table, it is not necessary to specify all of the column names in the parenthesis. It is possible to insert data in only specified columns by putting a select number of attributes in parentheses. For example, to insert attribute data for only AgentID and Height, this construction might be used:

INSERT INTO agent (AgentID, Height)

VALUES (10, 65);

 The values input here will be inserted into the appropriate spot on the table, and the other attributes in the table will be replaced with NULL.

 Looking back over the data, it looks like agent Pluto's height was not entered. However, since that attribute is allowed to have NULL values, this is fine. Take a look at the table created by entering these records. Query all the records from this data frame using the statement SELECT * FROM agent;, which should return the "agent" table:

```
Query:
  1  SELECT * FROM agent;
```

Results:

	agentid	agentname	height	haircolor	technology	intelligence	speed	communication	protection
1	1	Mars	77	Red	4	4	2	4	5
2	2	Neptune	72	Blue	5	3	5	1	2
3	3	Diana	64	Yellow	4	5	5	2	5
4	4	Minerva	60	Purple	4	5	1	5	3
5	5	Venus	61	Red	2	4	2	5	4
6	6	Pluto	null	Purple	4	4	4	4	4

 Success! We have created an agent table with all of our records!

Activity 4

Relational Databases

Does Jupiter care only about his agents and the types of skills they have? Of course not—the relationships between the agents, their missions, and what supplies they use are just as important. With these relationships and data in place, anyone using the database can query information about Mithras and the agents.

Though it would be possible to include all this additional information in a single table, having all that data in a single place would be confusing and not easy to look through. Anyone using the database would not be able to query efficiently. Instead, the solution is to create multiple tables that have defined relationships between them. In other words, the solution is a relational database.

It is now time to decide what tables to include in this relational database for Mithras. Jupiter wants information about the missions and what supplies were used on the missions. Therefore, there need to be tables linking the missions with their agents, the types of supplies that Mithras has, and what supplies were used on each mission and by which agents.

Start off by thinking about the missions table. Jupiter thinks the important attributes of each mission are the agent who went on the mission, what organization or person was the target, what country the mission was in, the latitude and longitude coordinates, and whether or not the mission was a success. With that in mind, the table can be created:

```
CREATE TABLE missions (
        MissionID char(5) NOT NULL UNIQUE,
        AgentID Int,
        Target varchar(50),
        Country carchar(25),
        Latitude float(8),
        Longitude float(8),
        Status char(7),
```

Everything here should look familiar, except perhaps the Latitude and Longitude attributes, which are assigned as floats. Because latitude and longitude coordinates have numbers on either side of a decimal point and they can be negative or positive, they need to be entered as a float, which includes those characteristics. Something like int, for example, would not allow the use of the decimal.

There should not be duplicate rows for each mission and corresponding agent in this table, because that could produce inaccurate results when the data is queried. Each table needs a primary key and a set of unique identifiers that define each record. If there are multiple identifiers, it is called a composite key. If there is one identifier, this is called a simple key. For the "missions" table, the PRIMARY KEY is defined by the MissionID. AgentID is identified as the PRIMARY KEY in the "agent" table, so here it will be assigned as a FOREIGN KEY and REFERENCE the agent table. The FOREIGN KEY constraint defines a column or combination of columns whose values match the PRIMARY KEY in the "agent" table:

```
CREATE TABLE missions (
        MissionID char(5) NOT NULL UNIQUE,
        AgentID int,
        Target varchar(50),
        Country varchar(25),
        Latitude float(8),
        Longitude float(8),
        Status char(7),
PRIMARY KEY(MissionID),
FOREIGN KEY (AgentID) REFERENCES agent
):
```

This is an example of a one-to-many relationship, because there can be many missions associated with a single agent. However, if multiple agents were allowed to go on each mission, then it would create a many-to-many relationship—where each agent goes on multiple missions and each mission has multiple agents.

Time to add in some information using the INSERT INTO statement.

```
INSERT INTO missions (MissionID, AgentID, Target, Country,
   Latitude, Longitude, Status)
VALUES
        ('M2356', 1, 'Nero', 'Italy', 41.986119, 12.339559, 'Success'),
        ('M3487', 1, 'Ice Castle', 'Croatia', 44.253886, 15.905702,
          'Failure'),
        ('M9876', 2, 'Caesar', 'Greece', 39.614200, 20.294604,
          'Success'),
        ('M3874', 4, 'Volcanic Mountain', 'France', 43.577784,
          5.821993, 'Success'),
        ('M8749', 4, 'Gaius', 'United States', 42.873463,
          -78.771570, 'Success'),
        ('M5886', 4, 'Zero Gravity', 'Canada', 49.259280,
          -123.162357, 'Failure'),
        ('M8932', 5, 'Tiberius', 'United States', 39.951653,
          -82.988848, 'Success');
```

That is a lot of information about missions—now it is time to create a table of supplies that Mithras has in its agency warehouse. Start off by assigning a SupplyID that will be the PRIMARY KEY for this table. It will also be useful to have a descriptive name, what category the supply falls under, the quantity that is available in the warehouse, and the cost per unit. As in the above tables, the table needs to be made with the CREATE command, then data will be populated using the INSERT INTO command:

```
CREATE TABLE supplies (
        SupplyID char(5) NOT NULL UNIQUE PRIMARY KEY,
        Name varchar(50),
        Quantity int,
        CostPerUnit float(8));

INSERT INTO supplies (SupplyID, Name, Category, Quantity,
  CostPerUnit)
VALUES
        ('A5592', 'Camera Glasses', 'Gadget', 20, 300.42),
        ('A6639', 'Data Scrambler', 'Gadget', 20, 1500.36),
        ('C9932', 'Surveillance Drone', 'Gadget', 10, 10321.43),
        ('D3399', 'Shrink Ray', 'Gadget', 1, 525255.67),
        ('A4456', 'Stun Wrist Watch', 'Gadget', 10, 233.54),
        ('C5563', 'Sonic Distractor', 'Gadget', 15, 569.23),
        ('A3424', 'Motorcycle', 'Transportation', 3, 10320.67),
        ('C4452', 'Yacht', 'Transportation', 2, 13200.56),
        ('D4398', 'Convertible', 'Transportation', 10, 88900.34),
        ('C9876', 'Helicopter', 'Transportation', 2, 267900.78),
        ('D5879', 'Wig', 'Disguise', 50, 125.23),
        ('B5478', 'Sunglasses', 'Disguise', 100, 52.78),
        ('D3291', 'Hat', 'Disguise', 75, 36.45);
```

Now that all the supply information is in place, check out what the table looks like by using the SELECT statement:

```
Query:
    1   SELECT * FROM supplies;

Results:
      supplyid  name               category        quantity  costperunit
 1    A5592     Camera Glasses     Gadget          20        300.42
 2    A6639     Data Scrambler     Gadget          20        1500.36
 3    C9932     Surveillance Drone Gadget          10        10321.4
 4    D3399     Shrink Ray         Gadget          1         525256
 5    A4456     Stun Wrist Watch   Gadget          10        233.54
 6    C5563     Sonic Distractor   Gadget          15        569.23
 7    A3424     Motorcycle         Transportation  3         10320.7
 8    C4452     Yacht              Transportation  2         132001
 9    D4398     Convertible        Transportation  10        88900.3
 10   C9876     Helicopter         Transportation  2         267901
 11   D5879     Wig                Disguise        50        125.23
 12   B5478     Sunglasses         Disguise        100       52.78
 13   D3291     Hat                Disguise        75        36.45
```

This is all fine, but the "supplies" table does not relate to the "agent" or "missions" tables. There should be a table that details the supplies used for each mission, including the AgentID, the MissionID, the SupplyID, and the quantity of the supplies. Try to figure out how to CREATE and INSERT data into a "missiondetails" table based on the following information:

AgentID	MissionID	SupplyID	QuantityUsed
1	M2356	A5592	1
1	M2356	D3291	8
1	M2356	A3424	1
2	M9876	A6639	1
2	M9876	D4398	1
2	M9876	B5478	5
2	M9876	C9932	2
4	M3874	A4456	1
4	M3874	C4452	1
4	M3874	C5563	4
4	M8749	D3399	1
4	M8749	C5563	1
4	M8749	C9876	1
4	M8749	A5592	1
5	M8932	A5592	1
5	M8932	D5879	3
5	M8932	D4398	2

What is the PRIMARY KEY for this table? Are there any FOREIGN KEYS? What are the data types? This will all be important for creating and inserting the table.

The final Mithras database schema looks like this:

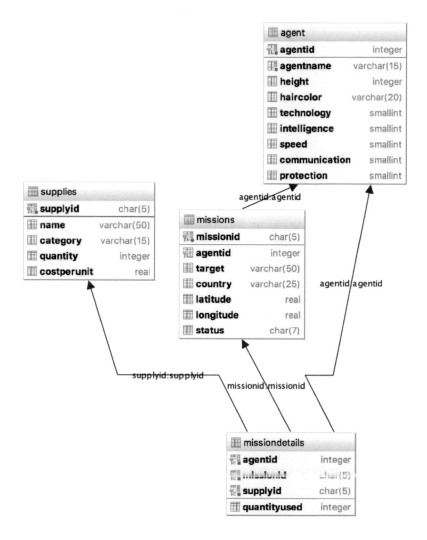

Activity 5

Altering and Dropping Tables

Things are happening at Mithras, and Jupiter needs information to be changed, updated, and added to the Mithras database.

First, Mithras just hired another agent: Mercury has passed his assessments and is now ready to officially join the organization. Agent Mercury has red hair, has a height of 63 inches, and scored a 5 in Technology, 2 in Intelligence, 5 in Speed, 5 in Communication, and 1 in Protection. Adding this new agent and his data into the database should be easy: just use the statement INSERT INTO again. Work on inserting agent Mercury into the agent table with the AgentID 7.

Next, agent Pluto was finally measured, and his height is 70 inches. To add this additional information to a row that already exists, use the UPDATE statement:

UPDATE agent
SET Height=70
WHERE AgentName='Pluto';

To break this down: the first line is used to UPDATE the "agent" table. The Height attribute in that table needs to be given a value of 70, which is added by using the SET statement. The SET statement is used with UPDATE to specify which attributes and values should be updated in the appropriate table. Finally, it is important to note that—without the WHERE command—these two lines would update every Height attribute to be valued at 70; that is not correct. This is why the WHERE statement is included—it tells the database that the only place in which the Height attribute should be changed is under agent Pluto's information.

Sadly, agent Diana has left Mithras, so she needs to be removed from the "agents" table. Luckily, she has not gone on any missions or used any supplies, so her records do not need to be removed from those tables. To remove her data, use the DELETE FROM statement to remove agent Diana from the agent table:

DELETE FROM agent WHERE AgentName='Diana';

Try replacing "WHERE AgentName= 'Diana'" with "WHERE AgentID=3" to see if the updated code produces the same result.

With the agents squared away, Jupiter needs mission date information to be added to the "missions" table. This means a new attribute column needs to be added to the table. Adding new attributes can be done by using the statement ALTER TABLE. This command allows users to delete, add, or modify an attribute in an existing table. The code for adding data about mission dates should look like this:

ALTER TABLE missions
ADD MissionDate date;

This code is telling the database that new information (the MissionDate attribute) is going to be added to the "missions" table. Following the ADD command and the attribute name is its type—in this case, date. The date data type can be used for day, month, and year information, but not time of day.

The table now has an added column with all NULL values—but Jupiter wanted to put the constraint that the new attribute cannot have a NULL value. To change this, it is necessary to DROP the attribute MissionDate, put the constraint NOT NULL, and then set a default value. The Mithras agency was founded on March 5, 2010, so that can be set as the default MissionDate. However, all of the mission dates should not stay as the default date—that would not be useful to Jupiter at all. To replace the default date with the actual MissionDate, the UPDATE statement will show up again. There are other, more complicated ways to do this using INSERT INTO and combining UPDATE statements together. Play around and see if you can figure them out.

```
ALTER TABLE missions
ADD MissionDate date;

ALTER TABLE missions
ADD MissionDate date;

ALTER TABLE missions
DROP COLUMN MissionDate;

ALTER TABLE missions
ADD MissionDate date NOT NULL
DEFAULT '2010-03-05';

UPDATE missions SET MissionDate='2014-01-06' WHERE
    missionid='M2356';
UPDATE missions SET MissionDate='2016-05-22' WHERE
    missionid='M3487;
UPDATE missions SET MissionDate='2017-01-18' WHERE
    missionid='M9876';
UPDATE missions SET MissionDate='2014-07-09' WHERE
    missionid='M3874';
UPDATE missions SET MissionDate='2015-09-24' WHERE
    missionid='M8749';
UPDATE missions SET MissionDate='2018-11-22' WHERE
    missionid='M5886';
UPDATE missions SET MissionDate='2019-05-02' WHERE
    missionid='M8932';
```

The "missions" table now has a column for a MissionDates attribute, and Jupiter's best database manager knows how to add, update, and alter information in the Mithras database.

Activity 6

Searching a Database with SELECT

Mithras now has a cutting-edge, up-to-date database. Jupiter wants to start using it. He is very busy, so he needs help querying the data and getting answers.

First, Jupiter wants to see all the agents and all their attributes in the agent table. Previously, the statement "SELECT * FROM agent;" was used to get an output of the entire table with all the attributes and records. The SELECT statement allows users to extract data from the agent table based on some criteria. SELECT *—using the asterisk or star after the SELECT statement—means the command is selecting all the attributes from the column. Jupiter now says that the table is too big and he really only wanted to see the AgentID along with the agent's Intelligence and Protection scores. A table including only those attributes can be produced using a statement like this:

SELECT * FROM agent;
SELECT AgentID, Intelligence, Protection FROM agent;

Using this basic concept and code format, try to query all of Jupiter's requests about information from the Mithras database. Jupiter's List:

- What types of supplies were used on the missions?
- Jupiter wants the MissionID, AgentID, Target, and Country for missions that were in the countries Croatia, France, and Canada.

- Jupiter wants the list of supplies in the Mithras warehouse that are not Gadgets.
- Jupiter wants the records where agents Minerva and Mars were on mission and whether or not the mission was a success. Jupiter wants this specific information saved in a new database in a table named "Magents."

For the first question, Jupiter is asking what supplies have been used on the missions. To get this information, it is necessary to extract which supply items have been used from the "missiondetails" table. This can be done by using the SELECT DISTINCT statement:

```
Query:
  1   SELECT DISTINCT SupplyID FROM missiondetails;

Results:
        supplyid
  1     C9876
  2     D3399
  3     B5478
  4     D4398
  5     D3291
  6     C4452
  7     A4456
  8     A5592
  9     D5879
  10    C9932
  11    C5563
  12    A3424
  13    A6639
```

This query reveals that there are seventeen supplies used in the entire "missiondetails" table—but only thirteen of the supplies are distinct.

In an earlier activity, the WHERE clause was used to filter the records for Pluto and Diana. To finish the rest of Jupiter's list, it is necessary to use the WHERE clause combined with an operator, such as AND, OR, IN, or NOT. The AND operator checks whether all of the conditions specified are true and then displays that record. The OR operator checks if at least one of the conditions specified is true. The IN operator allows users to specify multiple OR conditions without having to write out the attribute names individually. The NOT operator checks if a condition is not true and then displays those records.

For the second item on Jupiter's list, which operator should be used to select all records that have either Croatia, France, or Canada in the Country attribute? The operator should be OR for all of the records where at least one of the countries is Croatia, France, or Canada. Better yet, the IN operator will be even more efficient. For the third item on Jupiter's list, he wants a list of supplies that were anything except Gadgets. This means, of course, making use of the NOT operator.

The final bullet on Jupiter's list is a little more complicated. Jupiter wants to find out the AgentIDs for Minerva and Mars, query those AgentIDs from the "missions" table, only display the missions that were a success, and then save all that output into an entirely new table: "Magents." That is quite a lot of work.

The AgentID information for agent Minerva and agent Mars in the "agent" table—their AgentIDs are 1 and 4, respectively. The "missions" table now needs to be queried to show only the missions for AgentID 1 or AgentID 4—and the AND operator should be used to display only the successful missions for these two agents.

```
/* Jupiter wants the MissionID, AgentID, Target, and Country for
   missions that were in the countries Croatia, France, or Canada.
*/
/* Using the OR operator */
SELECT MissionID, AgentID, Target, Country FROM missions
WHERE Country='Croatia' OR Country='France' OR
   Country='Canada' ;


/*Using the IN operator */
SELECT MissionID, AgentID, Target, Country FROM missions
WHERE Country IN ('Croatia', 'France', 'Canada');


/* Jupiter wants the lists of supplies in the Mithras warehouse
   that are not Gadgets.
*/
SELECT * FROM supplies WHERE NOW Category='Gadget';


/* Jupiter wants the records where agents Minerva or Mars were
   on a mission and the mission was successful.
*/
/* Find AgentIDs for Minerva and Mars */
SELECT * FROM agent WHERE AgentName='Minerva' OR
   AgentName='Mars';
/* Select only the successful missions for agents Minerva or
   Mars */
SELECT *FROM missions WHERE (AgentID=1 OR AgentID=4)
   AND Status='Success';


/* Put the output in a new table called Magents */
SELECT MissionID, AgentID, Target, Country, Latitude,
   Longitude, Status, MissionDate
INTO Magents
FROM missions
WHERE (AgentID=1 OR AgentID=4) AND Status='Success';
```

In these final queries, notice that the AgentID attributes
for both the search subjects were put in parentheses. This

was done to indicate that the OR operator should be applied between these two agents—and not functioning with respect to the Status attribute. After extracting the records for the two agents, they are filtered by using the AND operator and specifying that the mission had to be a success.

To create the new table Magents, it is necessary to call out and select all the required attributes. Then, the INTO clause is used to specify the new table name ("Magents") and the FROM command specifies which table ("missions") this data is coming from. Finally, the WHERE command is used to filter the data so that it only shows up in the new table if it meets all the requirements—in this case, missions that involve agents Minerva or Mars; took place in Croatia, France, or Canada; and were successful.

Activity 7

Advanced Filtering Techniques

Always busy, Jupiter has now requested all the SupplyIDs and supply names that start with "A" or "C" and have a quantity in the warehouse greater than or equal to 10 and a cost per unit less than 1,000.

Unfortunately, it is not possible to filter the database by querying "WHERE SupplyID= 'A' OR SupplyID= 'C'" because this would not return anything. Because SupplyID attributes are made up of letters and numbers, it is necessary to use the LIKE operator with a WHERE statement to search for things in a character or string attribute that meet the search requirements. In this case, it is necessary to search for SupplyIDs that begin with either "A" or "C."

To do this, it is necessary to use something called a wildcard. A wildcard is used to substitute some character in a string. Before, the asterisk symbol was used as a wildcard to substitute all of the attribute names. Now, you need to use symbols to see if the character string for SupplyID matches a pattern.

The first supply item in the supplies table has the SupplyID A5592; check to see if certain patterns are present in that SupplyID.

What pattern?	Statement	True or False
The whole string	'A5592' LIKE 'A5592'	True
The first letter of the string	'A5592' LIKE 'A%'	True
The fourth character of the string	'A5592' LIKE '%9_'	True
The fourth character of the string	'A5592' LIKE '%5_'	False

The underscore character represents one character in a string. The percentage symbol represents either zero, one, or multiple characters in a string. To get only the supplies that start with "A" or "C," the command should look like:

WHERE SupplyID LIKE 'A%' OR SupplyID LIKE C%';

This will return a table like this:

```
Query:
  1    SELECT SupplyID, Name FROM supplies
  2    WHERE SupplyID LIKE 'A%' OR SupplyID LIKE   'C%';
Results:

       supplyid   name

  1    A5592      Camera Glasses

  2    A6639      Data Scrambler

  3    C9932      Surveillance Drone

  4    A4456      Stun Wrist Watch

  5    C5563      Sonic Distractor

  6    A3424      Motorcycle

  7    C4452      Yacht

  8    C9876      Helicopter
```

Jupiter also wanted to see only the supplies that have a quantity greater than or equal to 10 and a cost per unit less than 1,000. To determine which items meet these criteria, some new operators can be used:

- < (less than)
- > (greater than)
- <= (less than or equal to)
- >= (greater than or equal to)

These operators can be used in various combinations to filter data based on its numeric content, like so:

```
Query:
    select SupplyID, Name, Quantity, CostPerUnit FROM supplies
  2 WHERE (SupplyID LIKE 'A%' OR SupplyID LIKE  'C%') AND Quantity>=10 AND CostPerUnit <=1000;
Results:

    supplyid   name           quantity   costperunit
  1 A5592      Camera Glasses  20         300.42
  2 A4456      Stun Wrist Watch 10        233.54
  3 C5563      Sonic Distractor 15        569.23
```

Further filtering the data based on these two constraints, there are just three supplies that remain: Camera Glass, Stun Wrist Watch, and Sonic Distractor.

Jupiter reviewed the report and now wants to change the query to finding supplies with a per-unit between 1,000 and 150,000. Working with a range of numbers like this, it will be helpful to use the BETWEEN operator. BETWEEN allows users to select values that are between two limits. Here, the minimum value is 1,000 and the maximum value is 150,000, and the search needs to be completed within those boundaries:

```
Query:
    SELECT SupplyID, Name, Quantity, CostPerUnit FROM supplies
  2 WHERE (SupplyID LIKE 'A%' OR SupplyID LIKE  'C%') AND Quantity>=10 AND (CostPerUnit BETWEEN 1000 and 150000);
Results:

    supplyid   name            quantity   costperunit
  1 A6639      Data Scrambler   20         1500.36
  2 C9032      Surveillance Drone 10       10321.4
```

There are only two supplies that fall under this query: the Data Scrambler and the Surveillance Drone.

Activity 8

Aggregating Functions

Jupiter is meeting with a potential investor to get more money to fund the agency's missions. He needs a summary of the agent information to help him choose which agent should be sent on a mission for this investor. Jupiter has asked for answers to the following queries, which should be available through the "agents" table:

- The potential investor is really interested in the Intelligence scores of the agents; which agent scored the highest in that category?
- As a trial run, to complete a mission for the investor, Jupiter needs the shortest agent.
- Jupiter also needs to know how many agents have each hair color type.
- To summarize the skills of all of his agents, Jupiter would like to know the average of each skill among all agents.
- To help distinguish between the agents, Jupiter would like the sum of each agent's Technology, Intelligence, Speed, Communication, and Protection scores. Finally, Jupiter would like the scores to be arranged so the highest agent sum is at the top of the list and the lowest agent sum is on the bottom.

SQL has the functions MIN, MAX, SUM, AVG, and COUNT to deal with these types of requests.

For the first question, Jupiter would like the agent who is rated highest in Intelligence. One way to find this information is to define the maximum score possible in the Intelligence attribute and then list the name of the agent who meets that maximum. This can be done by using the MAX() function, which returns the largest value of the column:

```
SELECT AgentID, AgentName, Intelligence
   FROM agent
   WHERE Intelligence = (SELECT MAX(Intelligence) FROM
      agent);
```

This code first selects the attributes Jupiter is looking for—AgentID, AgentName, and Intelligence—from the agent table. Remember, a WHERE condition is searching for an attribute equal to something, where something can be a number, a character, or, in this case, a maximum value. Then these attributes are filtered by selecting the maximum Intelligence score.

The second question is asking for the shortest agent— or the agent who has the minimum height. Try finding the minimum height using the format above and replacing MAX with MIN. This will reveal the shortest agent.

Jupiter also needs to know how many people have which hair color. This means that he needs a frequency chart—or a count of each hair color that is in the "agent" table. Coming up with this chart will require a new variable: "Frequency." This variable will be based on each hair color's count. It is also necessary to group the data by the specific hair colors. Why? Try typing in "SELECT COUNT(HairColor) FROM agent;" to see what happens.

Needless to say, the results are not what Jupiter is looking for. The GROUP BY statement will do a better job; it bundles the results into one or more subsets. In this case, the results should be sorted by hair colors: red, purple, and blue. Using the code below produces the result that three agents have red hair, two agents have purple hair, and one agent has blue hair.

```
Query:
   1   SELECT HairColor, COUNT(HairColor)AS Frequency FROM agent
   2      GROUP BY HairColor;
Results:

     haircolor   frequency

  1  Red         3
  2  Purple      2
  3  Blue        1
```

Moving on to Jupiter's other requests, it is possible to average and sum attributes in a table by using the SUM and AVG functions. To get the average of each skill:

```
Query:
   SELECT avg(Technology) AS TechnologyAvg, avg(Intelligence) AS IntelligenceAvg, avg(Speed) AS SpeedAvg,
   2        avg(Communication) AS CommunicationAvg,avg(Protection) AS ProtectionAvg FROM agent;
Results:

   technologyavg        intelligenceavg       speedavg          communicationavg     protectionavg

 1 4.0000000000000000   3.6666666666666667   3.1666666666666667  4.0000000000000000   3.1666666666666667
```

In this code, the name of—for example—the resulting average of the Technology attribute is named TechnologyAvg. Renaming a product is done by adding AS between the function and the new name—so when the results come up, things are easier to recognize.

For Jupiter's final request, he needs to know the sum of each agent's skills. This is asking for an average of a record, or row, and not an average of an attribute, or column.

To sum a record, it is not possible to just use the SUM() function. Instead, a new sum function will be created by adding up all of the attributes by record and renaming that sum to a new variable in the table:

SELECT AgentID, AgentName, (Technology+ Intelligence+ Speed+ Communication+ Protection) AS AgentSkillSum
      FROM agent
      GROUP BY AgentID
      ORDER BY AgentSkillSum DESC;

This block of code needs some explanation. For starters, it is selecting the AgentID and the AgentName, then creating a new attribute—AgentSkillSum—that is just the addition of the skill attributes from the "agent" table. Like with count, since Jupiter wants a sum for every agent, it is necessary to GROUP BY agent. Finally, to get the highest sum first, the ORDER BY statement is used to sort the new data by AgentSkillSum. DESC means the results are sorted in descending order (while ASC would mean to sort the data in ascending order).

	agentid	agentname	agentskillsum
1	6	Pluto	20
2	1	Mars	19
3	4	Minerva	18
4	7	Mercury	18
5	5	Venus	17
6	2	Neptune	16

From the output, it is plain to see that Pluto has the highest skill sum and Neptune has the lowest skill sum. Based on this information, which agent should Jupiter send on this mission for the potential investor?

Activity 9

Relationships, Efficiency, and Speed

Jupiter loves the Mithras database's efficiency and speed. However, it still has room to improve. Instead of having to query the "agent" table to find AgentIDs that could help run a query on the "missions" table, for example, it would be better to just combine those two tables so the search could be run all at once.

The good news is that it is not too difficult to make this change. The solution lies in forging relationships between the tables in a database through PRIMARY KEYS and FOREIGN KEYS. Even though AgentID is the unique PRIMARY KEY in the "agent" table, it is also referenced in the "missions" table and the "missiondetails" table. SupplyID is the PRIMARY KEY in the "supplies" table, but it also is in the "missiondetails" table.

Tables can be merged together based on the relationships between them and what outcome is desired. The JOIN command in SQL combines rows between two or more tables based on the similar attributes between them. For example: say AgentName should be added to the "missions" to get more information about which agents have completed which assignments. Remember that each agent can have more than one mission, so there is a one-to-many relationship between these two tables. Use the RIGHT JOIN clause to join the "agent" table and "missions" table together. Take a look at the image below; the "missions" table is represented in blue on the right, and the "agent" table is represented in red on the left. The RIGHT JOIN clause returns all of the records from the "missions" table and the matched records from the "agent" table.

Now, since it is only necessary to focus on the AgentName and the attribute or key that links the two tables together— the AgentID—it is possible to select only those two attributes from the "agent" table. How does one select attributes from more than one table? The general format to specify that a variable is coming from a table is to type the table name, a period, and then the attribute. For example, AgentName from the "agent" table becomes:

agent.AgentName

It is also possible to select all of the attributes from a table by typing the table name, a period, and then an asterisk. Since this example will use all the attributes for missions:

select missions.*

Here is an example code block for a RIGHT JOIN that merges the "agent" and "missions" tables:

```
SELECT agent.AgentName, agent.AgentID, missions.*
FROM agent
RIGHT JOIN missions
ON agent.AgentID = missions.AgentID;
```

The ON statement here specifies which attributes to link between the tables. In this case, the AgentID variables are being connected. In the final output, each agent's AgentID attribute is included and shown without having to create a separate query:

agentname	agentid	missionid	agentid	target	country	latitude	longitude	status	missiondate
Mars	1	M2356	1	Nero	Italy	41.9861	12.3396	Success	"2014-01-06"
Mars	1	M3487	1	Ice Castle	Croatia	44.2539	15.9057	Failure	"2016-05-22"
Neptune	2	M9876	2	Caesar	Greece	39.6142	20.2946	Success	"2017-03-18"
Minerva	4	M3874	4	Volcanic Mountain	France	43.5778	5.82199	Success	"2014-07-09"
Minerva	4	M8749	4	Gaius	United States	42.0735	-78.7716	Success	"2016-09-24"
Minerva	4	M5886	4	Zero Gravity	Canada	49.2593	-123.162	Failure	"2018-11-22"
Venus	5	M8932	5	Tiberius	United States	39.9517	-82.9888	Success	"2019-05-02"

What about including information from the "supplies" table into the "missiondetails" table? The LEFT JOIN keyword phrase mirrors the RIGHT JOIN command. LEFT JOIN returns all records from the left table and the matched records from the right table. Let "missiondetails" be the left table and "supplies" be the right table for this example. The goal here is to match the attributes in the "missiondetails" table and the attributes SupplyID, Name, and CostPerUnit in the "supplies" table. Try matching "missiondetails" and "supplies" using LEFT JOIN by the attribute SupplyID.

There are other types of JOIN commands, as well, including FULL JOIN, INNER JOIN, and UNION. FULL JOIN takes all records from the left and the right tables when there is a match based on some attributes and fills in NULL for any unmatched attributes. INNER JOIN does the opposite, taking only the cases that matched in the left and right tables and not returning anything that does not match. Finally, UNION joins two or more SELECT statements into one if they have the same data types.

Activity 10

Sub-Setting Data for Specific Mission Needs

Jupiter is trying to figure out how costly agents Minerva, Pluto, and Venus are for the agency compared to their success rate. Additionally, a lot has happened in the last few weeks and the Mithras database needs to be updated.

Agents Minerva, Pluto, and Venus have all gone on missions in the past week, so that data needs to be inserted in the "missions" table:

MissionID	AgentID	Target	Country	Latitude	Longitude	Status	MissionDate
M8862	4	Thunder Road	China	30.272455	120.10601	Success	8/11/19
M2381	5	Ancient Circus	India	19.09642	72.89081	Failure	8/9/19
M1111	6	Augustus	Brazil	-12.801756	-38.3667	Success	8/6/19

To assess how much money was spent on supplies, Jupiter needs to know what supplies the agents used on the missions—so that information should be added to the "missiondetails" table.

Minerva used a Data Scrambler, a Stun Wrist Watch, four Wigs, two Sunglasses, and a Convertible. Pluto used a Helicopter, two Hats, and two Surveillance Drones. Venus used a one pair of Camera Glasses, a Convertible, a Stun Wrist Watch, five Wigs, and three Sunglasses. Insert these records into the table "missiondetails."

Now that all of the information has been updated, it is time to create a table that has all of the information Jupiter needs to answer his question. First, the CostPerUnit variable from the "supplies" table will come in handy to calculate how much money each of the agents spent. JOIN the attributes CostPerUnit and Name from supplies with the "missiondetails" table with SupplyID. Remember that it is only necessary to include missions from agent Minerva, agent Pluto, and agent Venus. SELECT only the missions for these agents and create a new table from the "missiondetails" and "supplies" joined data. Call this new table "agentfinances."

Next, create a new variable that is a cost per quantity of supply item that each agent used. This can be done by multiplying CostPerUnit by QuantityUsed in the new table. Call this variable "CostPerQuant." Finally, each agent's total cost can be calculated:

agentid	total_agent_cost
4	1019777.86489868
5	467093.338150024
6	90218.7937698364

Agent 4 (Minerva) spent $1,019,777.86 across her missions. Agent 5 (Venus) spent $467,093.34 across her missions. Agent 6 (Pluto) spent $90,218.79 across his missions. Try figuring out the cost per mission or the average cost. Are the successful missions more expensive than the failed missions?

Career Connections

Complex databases are used all over the modern world. Banks use databases to keep track of accounts, balances, loans, and deposits. Retail stores use databases to store customer information, preferences, items in a shopping cart, and items people click on. Many entertainment venues and restaurants have applications that allow users to store personal information, credit card information, and purchase items. This information is saved as a record for that organization. Databases are used everywhere and for anyone that wants to store data, retrieve data, or analyze data.

These exercises deal with a small amount of data, entered by hand, to help understand the basics of databases. Even this foundational knowledge—of how to build a database from scratch, insert relationships between tables, extract records and information based on conditions, and create new tables for a specific goal—is important. With small quantities, it is easy to look at tables and come up with an answer without writing any SQL statements. In reality—with the rise of big data—information exists in enormous volumes. For example, think of how many items are in a store. A store's supply table could have thousands or millions of records. How can people easily extract what they want from that table without computational help?

Very large amounts of data are collected for every domain, and this data needs to be stored efficiently and in an organized manner specific to the purpose of that database. A quick online search can reveal dozens of open-source databases that contain millions of pieces of data. That data can be used to form questions, answer those questions, and make meaningful decisions about everyday life. No matter

Databases contain millions of pieces of data that can be used to both form questions and answer questions.

the type of database you use—relational, in the case of these activities—or type of database environment—such as PostgreSQL—the use and success of the database depends on how it is designed and implemented. If data is stored in an unorganized or nonstandard way, it will be hard to efficiently query data to be able to make any necessary decisions.

Relational databases, made up of multiple tables and their relationships, are used every day to mine data, select specific tables, and sift through aggregated information. For example, chief medical officers may want to find data on all of the doctors working for them, the diagnoses of the patients that they treat, and the procedures that they do for the patients. All of this data would be stored across multiple tables and must be queried and joined together so that meaningful information can be produced. Therefore, the more you hone your skills and understand the basics of database design and manipulation, the more prepared you will be to work

Good database design promotes good business. Data can be manipulated and queried to help company leaders make good, informed decisions.

with databases at many different levels within any major organization—regardless of the industry.

Since data science, big data, and databases are everywhere, there are many ways to use database skills in different job applications. There are database developers, designers, and administrators, all of whom have an important role to play in creating, designing, and maintaining a database and its applications. Database analysts develop databases for reporting based on decisions from the data. Database architects design and implement data management systems, while database consultants help the companies that have databases implemented to use the database technologies to improve their processes and achieve goals.

In addition, database design and management can tie into many other career paths. A data scientist uses methods, processes, and algorithms to extract data and find patterns and insights from data to influence changes. Statisticians and engineers use databases to store the data they use for analysis. For any career related to research, health, or technology, there will inevitably come a time to extract and use information from a database. Therefore, whether your future includes medicine, finance, retail, insurance firms, or marketing, you will use databases—and a fundamental understanding of their structure and function will be an enormous advantage.

Answer Key

Activity 4 Answer:

```
CREATE TABLE missiondetails (
AgentID int,
MissionID char(5),
        SupplyID char(5),
        QuantityUsed int,
        PRIMARY KEY (AgentID, MissionID, SupplyID),
        FOREIGN KEY (AgentID) REFERENCES agent,
        FOREIGN KEY (MissionID) REFERENCES missions,
        FOREIGN KEY (SupplyID) REFERENCES supplies,
);

INSERT INTO missiondetails (AgentID, MissionID, SupplyID,
  QuantityUsed)
VALUES
        (1, 'M2356', 'A5592', 1),
        (1, 'M2356', 'D3291', 8),
        (1, 'M2356', 'A3424', 1),
        (2, 'M9876', 'A6639', 1),
        (2, 'M9876', 'D4398', 1),
        (2, 'M9876', 'B5478', 5),
        (2, 'M9876', 'C9932', 2),
        (4, 'M3874', 'A4456', 1),
        (4, 'M3874', 'C4452', 1),
        (4, 'M3874', 'C5563', 4),
        (4, 'M8749', 'D3399', 1),
        (4, 'M8749', 'C5563', 1),
        (4, 'M8749', 'C9876', 1),
        (4, 'M8749', 'A5592', 1),
        (5, 'M8932', 'A5592', 1),
        (5, 'M8932', 'D5879', 3),
        (5, 'M8932', 'D4398', 2);
```

Activity 5 Answer:

/* Add agent Mercury to Agent Table */

INSERT INTO agent (AgentID, AgentName, Height, HairColor,
   Technology, Intelligence, Speed, Communication, Protection)
VALUES (7, 'Mercury', 63, 'Red', 5, 2, 5, 5, 1);

Activity 8 Answer:

SELECT AgentID, AgentName, Height FROM agent
WHERE Height = (SELECT MIN(Height) FROM agent);

The agent with the minimum height is Minerva.

Activity 9 Answer:

SELECT supplies.SupplyID, supplies.Name, supplies.CostPerUnit,
   missiondetails.*
FROM missiondetails
LEFT JOIN supplies
ON missiondetails.SupplyID = supplies.SupplyID
ORDER BY AgentID ASC;

Activity 10 Answer:

/* Create New Missions Table for the Three New Missions */
INSERT INTO missions (MissionID, AgentID, Target, Country,
   Latitude, Longitude, Status, MissionDate)
VALUES
        ('M8862', 4, 'Thunder Road', 'China', 30.272455,
           120.106013, 'Success', '2019-08-11'),
        ('M2381', 5, 'Ancient Circus', 'India', 19.09642, 72.89081,
           'Failure', '2019-08-09'),
        ('M1111', 6, 'Augustus', 'Brazil', –12.801756, –38.366700,
           'Success', '2019-08-06');

```
/* Find out what the SupplyIDs are for the Names */
SELECT SupplyID, Name FROM supplies
WHERE Name IN ('Data Scrambler', 'Stun Wrist Watch',
  'Wig','Sunglasses', 'Convertible', 'Helicopter', 'Hat',
  'Surveillance Drone', 'Camera Glasses');


/* Add the Supply data for the missions */
INSERT INTO missiondetails (AgentID, MissionID, SupplyID,
  QuantityUsed)
VALUES
        (4, 'M8862', 'A6639', 1),
        (4, 'M8862', 'A4456', 1),
        (4, 'M8862', 'D5879', 4),
        (4, 'M8862', 'B5478', 2),
        (4, 'M8862', 'D4398', 1),
        (5, 'M2381', 'C9876', 1),
        (5, 'M2381', 'D3291', 2),
        (5, 'M2381', 'C9932', 2),
        (6, 'M1111', 'A5592', 1),
        (6, 'M1111', 'D4398', 1),
        (6, 'M1111', 'A4456', 1),
        (6, 'M1111', 'D5879', 5),
        (6, 'M1111', 'B5478', 3);


/* Create a new table */
SELECT supplies.SupplyID, supplies.Name, supplies.CostPerUnit,
  missiondetails.MissionID, missiondetails.QuantityUsed,
  missiondetails.AgentID
INTO agentfinances
FROM supplies
LEFT JOIN missiondetails ON missiondetails.SupplyID =
  supplies.SupplyID
WHERE AgentID=4 OR AgentID=5 OR AgentID=6
ORDER BY AgentID ASC;
```

```
/* Create the New Variable CostPerQuant */
SELECT AgentID,MissionID, SupplyID, Name,QuantityUsed,
   CostPerUnit, QuantityUsed * CostPerUnit AS CostPerQuant
INTO agentfinancesquant
FROM agentfinances;

/* Find the sum of CostPerQuant for each agent */
SELECT AgentID, SUM(CostPerQuant) as Total_Agent_Cost
FROM agentfinancesquant
GROUP BY AgentID
ORDER BY AgentID ASC;
```

Glossary

attribute A column in a table that corresponds to a feature or variable that is trying to measure or describe something about a record.

constraint A restriction put on data, typically expressed in rules; NOT NULL, NULL, UNIQUE.

data Facts that have not been analyzed or processed.

database A structure that stores data related to some topic in an organized way.

database design The process of creating a structure that data and metadata will be stored in.

database management system (DBMS) Software for creating, managing, and retrieving information from databases.

data type A category that defines what kind or values an attribute can take.

foreign key An attribute in a table that references an attribute in another table.

information Processed data that reveals a meaning or pattern.

join To merge two data tables together.

many-to-many Describing one instance in a table that has a relationship with multiple instances in another table and one instance in the second table that has a relationship with multiple instances in the first table.

metadata Data about data characteristics and relationships.

one-to-many Describing one instance in a table that has a relationship with multiple instances in another table.

one-to-one Describing one instance in a table that only has a relationship with one instance in a second table.

primary key An attribute in a table that uniquely defines each record in the table.

query A search of a database done to extract data that can be processed into information.

record A row in a table that corresponds to an entry and the information about that entry.

relational database Multiple tables that have defined associations between them.

schema A logical depiction of a database, including tables, relationships, and constraints.

structured data Information that consists of numerical facts, data that can be organized on a scale, or data that can be organized in categories.

unstructured data Information that is not easily searchable, such as images and videos.

For More Information

Codecademy
575 Broadway, 5th floor
New York, NY 10012
Website: www.codecademy.com
Facebook and Twitter: @Codecademy
This online resource offers courses in dozens of
    programming languages, including SQL.

Data.gov
Website: https://catalog.data.gov/dataset
Twitter: @usdatagov
Data.gov contains more than 200,000 open datasets on
    many fields of interest, including climate, consumers,
    education, finance, health, and agriculture.

Digital Health Canada
1100–151 Yonge Street
Toronto, ON M5C 2W7
Canada
647-775-8555
Website: https://digitalhealthcanada.com
Facebook: @digitalhealthcdn
Instagram: @digitalhealth_canada
Twitter: @DigiHealthCA
Digital Health Canada is a professional organization that
    focuses on advancing digital initiatives—including
    complex database management—in health fields.

Informatica
2100 Seaport Boulevard
Redwood City, CA 94063
(650) 385-5000
Website: https://www.informatica.com
Facebook and Twitter: @Informatica
Informatica is a leading database management company,
   and its website features blogs and further information
   about the uses and benefits of databases in the
   modern world.

Open Government Portal
90 Elgin Street, 8th Floor
Ottawa, ON K1A 0R5
Canada
Website: https://open.canada.ca/data/en/dataset
Twitter: @OpenGovCanada
The Canadian Open Government Portal makes machine-
   readable data on many topics—such as art, music, and
   literature—available and easy to access.

PostgreSQL
Website: https://www.postgresql.org
Twitter: @PostgreSQL
PostgreSQL is an open source object-relational database
   system that uses the SQL language and other features
   to store and scale complex data. The development
   team's website features news, updates, and answers to
   countless SQL questions.

For Further Reading

Bella, Laura. *Becoming a Data Engineer*. New York, NY: Rosen YA, 2018.

Chen, Daniel Y. *Pandas for Everyone: Python Data Analysis*. Boston, MA: Addison-Wesley, 2018.

Fowler, Adam. *NoSQL for Dummies*. Hoboken, NJ: John Wiley & Sons, 2015.

Haider, Murtaza. *Getting Started with Data Science: Making Sense of Data with Analytics*. Boston, MA: IBM Press, Pearson, 2016.

Harris, Patricia. *Understanding Coding with Python*. New York, NY: Rosen Publishing, 2017.

Mooney, Carla and Alexis Cornell. *Big Data: Information in the Digital World with Science Activities for Kids*. White River Junction, VT: Nomad Press, 2018.

Mozer, Mindy. *Big Data and You*. New York, NY: Rosen Central, 2015.

Payment, Simone. *Getting to Know Python*. New York, NY: Rosen Central, 2015.

Bibliography

Bohlouli, Mahdi, et al. "Towards an Integrated Platform for Big Data Analysis." In *Integration of Practice-Oriented Knowledge Technology: Trends and Prospectives*, edited by Madjid Fathi, 47–56. Berlin, Germany: Springer, 2013.

Coronel, Carlos, Steven Morris, and Peter Rob. *Database Systems: Design, Implementation, and Management*. Boston, MA: Cengage Learning, 2013.

Kriegel, Alex. *Discovering SQL: A Hands-On Guide for Beginners*. Hoboken, NJ: John Wiley & Sons, 2011.

Takahashi, Mana and Shoko Azuma. *The Manga Guide to Databases*. San Francisco, CA: No Starch Press, 2009.

Taylor, Allen G. *SQL for Dummies*. Hoboken, NJ: John Wiley & Sons, 2018.

Index

About the Author

Sarah Mullin is a PhD student and educator in biomedical informatics, a field that studies the effective uses of biomedical data, information, and knowledge for scientific research, problem-solving, and decision-making in the medical domain. She has a master of science degree in statistics and loves designing databases in a practical way for predictive machine learning analytic use. She holds the longtime belief that well-designed databases and data can help create better research and influence health care outcomes in a positive way.

Photo Credits

Cover Joe Techapanupreeda/Shutterstock.com; cover, p. 1 (code) © iStockphoto.com/scanrail; p. 5 seewhatmitchsee/ Shutterstock.com; p. 6 Timofeev Vladimir/Shutterstock.com; p. 8 Asnia/Shutterstock.com; pp. 10, 17, 19, 23, 25, 30, 35, 36, 37, 40 (both), 41, 43, 44, 47 Sarah Mullin; p. 49 Drazen_/E+/ Getty Images; p. 50 Gorodenkoff/Shutterstock.com; interior pages border design © iStockphoto.com/Akrain.

Design: Matt Cauli; Editor: Siyavush Saidian; Photo researcher: Sherri Jackson